INTRODUCTION

Exciting historical texts for children are rare things. This is not because there is a lack of scholarly research in the field, nor is it because scholars do not recognise the fact that learning must have a base. It is due mainly to the inability of scholars to write in a language simple and attractive enough to appeal to children. Dan Fulani's text is an exception.

As fiction may be used to mirror what goes on in a society, so may a narrative syle be used to convey historical facts. The adventures of **Janjo** and **Shika** in **The Battle for Mombasa** fall into this category. Conscious of the elusive mood of his readers - juniors in scholarship - the author presents history through the eyes of Janjo, a typical African boy, and his lovable pet, Shika the monkey. Throughout the book, beautiful colour illustrations enhance the thrilling adventure, giving the child a visual interpretation of the true story. Maps have been appropriately used to illustrate the geographical locations pinpointed in the text, while the cleverly used fact boxes highlight the essential historical details, providing the young reader with a valuable key with which to discover knowledge.

Dan Fulani has used simple, clear sentences to narrate the saga of the fall of Fort Jesus in a fascinating style. He demonstrates the ability to interpret and summarise historical facts in a manner which will appeal to young readers. Without doubt, this will create a curiosity in the junior scholar to explore the world of African history in an inquiring and lively manner.

To conclude, this book brilliantly blends the two primary objectives of education and entertainment.

Professor D. M. Misra
Department of History, Kenyatta University
Nairobi, Kenya

For Pippa with love

Text by Dan Fulani
Edited by Bridget A. C. King
Illustrations by Patrick Kirby
Graphic Design by Katherine Mamai and Susan Scull-Carvalho
Published by JACARANDA DESIGNS LIMITED P.O. Box 76691 Nairobi, Kenya
Text copyright Dan Fulani, 1995
Series concept, illustrations and characters copyright (c) JACARANDA DESIGNS LIMITED
First published in 1995
ISBN 9966-884-99-8

Typeset in Friz Quadrata, MacHumaine and Revue. Colour separations and printing by Singapore National Printers.

JANJO and SHIKA

The Battle for Mombasa
(1696 - 1698)

Dan Fulani
Illustrated by Patrick Kirby

"You're not paying attention, Janjo. You'll never pass your history exam this way." The Headmaster leant over Janjo's shoulder and looked down at Janjo's empty exercise book. "As a punishment for wasting my time, I want you to do an extra homework essay on the Battle for Mombasa."

Janjo sighed. He hated history. Now he had more work to do. "It's not fair, Shika," he complained to his pet monkey as they strolled home after school. "What can I say that's interesting about an ancient old ruin like Fort Jesus?"

Shika scratched his ear in sympathy. He didn't like it when Janjo was miserable. It meant no fun for him.

When he reached his home, Janjo went straight into his bedroom to do his homework. His father was always cross if he left it until after supper, and when Janjo's father was cross, life was even less worth living.

"Right, Shika, I'm going to do exactly half an hour's work on this essay. If I set my watch properly, the alarm will ring after thirty minutes." Janjo fiddled with the digital watch which he'd been given as a birthday present. He still didn't know exactly how to set it. Shika sat on his shoulder and watched with a puzzled frown as Janjo pressed all the buttons at once. Suddenly...

"Hey Shika! What's happening? The date on my watch has changed. It's making a whirring sound. Help! I'm falling…"

Janjo's voice faded away. For a moment everything went black…

"Are you all right, Shika? Where are we? Wait a minute, I recognize that building. It's Fort Jesus. What's happened to us?"

Shika jumped up and down, squealing and pointing in the direction of the Fort. Three strangely dressed soldiers were striding towards them with old-fashioned muskets in their hands.

"Don't you know it's dangerous to be outside the Fort at this time?" demanded a mean-faced soldier, gripping Janjo's collar and pulling him to his feet.

"What are you doing here, boy?" asked another soldier more kindly.

"Let's take him and the monkey to the Fort. If the boy's a spy, the Captain will deal with him," said the third soldier with a cruel laugh.

Janjo and Shika were marched into the Fort through huge wooden gates covered with brass studs. They crossed the central courtyard and the unpleasant soldier knocked on the office door of the Captain, Joao Rodrigues.

"What is it, Gaston? I'm busy," the Captain growled as the soldiers entered.

"We've caught this boy and his monkey outside the Fort, Captain. What do you want us to do with them?" asked Gaston, the mean-faced soldier.

Captain Rodrigues looked up at Janjo and his bored expression turned to one of amazement. "What sort of a boy are you? Where have you come from?" he asked.

"Please, sir," Janjo said trembling. "I'm not a spy. Shika, my monkey, and I have landed here unexpectedly from the future. We don't know how to get home." Janjo had spotted the date 27th March 1696 on a calendar behind the Captain. He remembered dimly from his history lesson that this was the year there was some kind of trouble in the Fort. It didn't seem a good time to arrive.

"Another refugee with a crazy story," sighed Captain Rodrigues. "As if I haven't enough vagabonds with the entire population of Mombasa sheltering inside these walls. Are you Muslim or Christian?"

"I'm Christian, sir," Janjo replied.

"Take them both down to the kitchen, Gaston. The boy can help Manuel prepare food and draw water from the well. Just you behave yourself while you're here, boy, and see that your monkey doesn't get up to any mischief."

FORT JESUS

Now a museum, Fort Jesus stands on the island of Mombasa, in the Indian Ocean off the coast of Kenya. The Christian Portuguese built the Fort to protect their ships from the Moslem Turks who threatened their trading routes. Work on the Fort began in 1592 and took over twenty years to complete. The architect was John Baptist Cairatto. Huge stone building blocks were brought ready cut from Portugal. The labourers came from Malindi, further along the coast to the north and the stone-masons came from India. The Fort was designed in the shape of a Roman cross and planned so that cannon on the outer walls could defend the approaches from all sides. It was built on solid coral rock with one side facing the sea, another the wild bush, and the main gates facing the town of Mombasa and the road to the harbour. Three wells were dug within its walls to help withstand a siege.

It was just beginning to get dark as the soldiers led Janjo and Shika towards the huge kitchens. As they walked beside the walls, Shika pointed excitedly towards a strange figure standing alone on the ramparts.

"What's that up there?" Janjo asked Pablo pointing to the figure on the wall of the Fort.

"That's a wooden carving of Saint Anthony. We've dressed him up to look like a Portuguese soldier to fool the Omanis. When Fort Joseph on the other side of Mombasa was captured, we brought the Saint here. We believe that if he ever falls off the wall we're doomed," replied Pablo gloomily.

Everyone in the Fort was very superstitious about the statue and firmly believed that their fate rested on it remaining upright on top of the battlements of the Fort.

"Come on boy, stop dawdling," barked Gaston. "You've got work to do."

OMANI ARABS

In 1624 the Yarubi Dynasty came to power in Oman. In 1650 Sultan bin Seif, nephew of the powerful Imam, Nasir bin Murshid, finally overcame the Portuguese in Muscat. With speed and the help of the coastal people of the Persian Gulf he turned Oman into a powerful maritime power. By 1652 the Omanis were invited by the Kings of Zanzibar, Pemba and Otondo, to help them fight the Portuguese. From that time, the Omanis and the Portuguese ran a constant series of battles over the ownership of Fort Jesus, Zanzibar and Mozambique. Finally on 15th March they sailed forcefully into Kilindini channel. Fort St. Joseph immediately came under heavy fire and the garrison of four Portuguese and 250 citizens of Mombasa retreated to join the stronger force in Fort Jesus. They took with them the statue of Saint Anthony.

HOW THE SIEGE OF FORT JESUS BEGAN

The siege began on 15th March 1696 when the Omani fleet sailed into Mombasa waters with seven warships and ten dhows. When the terrified people of the town saw this, 2,500 men, women and children crowded into Fort Jesus for safety. Only about fifty were Portuguese, the rest were Arabs and Africans. The Fort contained only basic stores for the garrison and, despite the three wells, water for such a large crowd was constantly in short supply. The threat of starvation and thirst hung over the inmates and the Captain was very worried about the situation.

Shika clung on to Janjo's neck in fright as they entered the hot, smoky kitchen. to be confronted by flying feathers and the noise of clattering pots and pans. The last scrawny survivor of a coop of live chickens was trying to avoid being caught by a little dark-haired man with a long drooping moustache who was chasing the chicken around a table clutching a butcher's knife.

"Come here you stupid chicken," panted the little man. "Come and get your miserable neck rung."

Gaston ignored him and went over to the chief cook, an imposingly large man wearing a dirty, white apron around his vast stomach. Steam from two enormous pots of boiling water had made his round, red face shiny with sweat.

"The Captain's sent these two to help you. Put them to work and make sure they keep out of mischief." So saying, Gaston turned on his heel and marched away, leaving Janjo and Shika staring up at the huge cook in dismay.

"Madonna! Are we so desperate we need to eat monkey now?" he exclaimed throwing up his hands in horror. Shika squealed and tried to hide inside Janjo's shirt. "Manuel, leave that miserable chicken alone and come here. Take this boy to the well and bring back some more water."

"We haven't eaten curried monkey—yet," Manuel said waving his knife menacingly over Shika's tail where it hung out of Janjo's shirt. "It's a pity it's not big enough to feed more than two people."

"Don't touch my monkey!" Janjo cried. "Don't you dare touch him or I'll…"

Janjo never finished the sentence. The kitchen doors were suddenly flung open with a crash and a robed Franciscan friar burst into the room. "The Omanis have cut the cables of the supply ships. Quickly! Come and help or we'll lose all our supplies."

Janjo and Shika ran up to the top of the of the wall of the Fort with the rest of the kitchen staff. They watched helplessly as the galliots carrying the Fort's supplies drifted slowly out to sea.

"Look out! They're firing on us," shouted a soldier.

"There goes our precious food!" moaned the chief cook in despair.

"Now we're really in trouble," Manuel muttered.

"I've an idea," whispered Janjo to Shika. Dodging through the onlookers he ran down a long row of stone steps which led towards the beach. The door at the end of the steps was barred, but the stones in the wall looked insecure and not too well cemented together. "Help me, Shika," he urged, trying to work a big stone loose. "If we can make a small hole in the wall, you can get through and throw a rope from one of the ships. Then we can all try to drag it ashore."

Shika leapt down from Janjo's shoulder and was soon helping him dig out the crumbling mortar around the stones with his sharp fingers. They managed to work a large stone free and with one great push, it fell to the ground. The hole it left was small, but just big enough for Shika to crawl through.

"See that palm tree leaning over in the wind?" Janjo said. "If you climb that you can jump on to the ship's rigging. Tie a rope firmly round the mast. By that time I'll be on the beach and you can throw me the rope." Shika chattered excitedly as he squeezed through the hole and sped off across the sand towards the tall, swaying palm tree on the beach. Janjo worked frantically to shift a few more stones from the wall and then called out to the crowd: "Over here! Come and help me!"

GALLIOT

A fully rigged ship capable of carrying troops and crew into battle. They were also used to carry supplies from Goa to feed the besieged inhabitants of the Fort.

Five spectators turned to each other, nodded, and ran down the steps just in time to see Janjo disappear through the hole in the wall. They squeezed through after him and once they reached the beach they immediately understood Janjo's plan. Running over to Janjo, they watched as Shika scrambled half-way up the mainmast and attempted to throw a rope towards them. The heavy rope fell short and splashed into the sea but one of the men plunged into the water and grabbed the rope before it was drawn back by the waves.

Slinging the rope over their shoulders, they began to pull with all their might. "Heave! Heave!," they shouted in unison. Refugees, soldiers, monks and kitchen staff all grabbed hold of the rope. Slowly the ship began to move towards the shore.

"Heave! Heave! Heave!"

"Help! Help! Help!" cried Manuel who was dangling helplessly, his short legs kicking in the air as the rope was lifted higher by taller men.

"Heave!" cried the crowd in unison.

"Help!" cried Manuel again. "I want to go back to Oporto!" He let go of the rope and disappeared under the water with a splash.

The ship was finally pulled ashore and the crowd swarmed on board to rescue the cargo of sacks, barrels and chests containing food and other valuable necessities.

"Hurry!" cried Janjo. "The Omanis haven't seen us yet. We must hurry."

"The sun's coming up. Hurry, men," Pablo called out as he rolled a barrel over the sand.

Someone laid a sack of flour on Manuel's head for him to carry. It split, covering the little cook in white powder.

"I am cooked," spluttered Manuel. "I am an Omani omelette."

Shika and Janjo burst out laughing.

"Come on, Shika, give me a hand with this chest, and let's get back inside the Fort. The Omanis must have spotted us by now and I don't want to end up on the point of their curved daggers."

°⁄△▽⋀▽⋀▽△\°

When all the supplies salvaged from the galliot had been safely stored away, the Captain sent for Janjo and Shika. "Well done," he said shaking Shika's paw and smiling at Janjo. "Thanks to your bravery, we've salvaged enough food for another few weeks. However, we're still in a desperate position so I'm going to ask you to help us again. I want you to sail to Zanzibar Island to ask the Queen of Zanzibar for help. She's a good friend of the Portuguese and I'm sure I can count on her to send us supplies. It's a dangerous mission, but despite your youth and strange appearance you've proved yourselves worthy."

"We'll try, but how do we get there?" asked Janjo.

"You'll have to take an Arab dhow from the harbour. I'll send three soldiers and a sailor with you. You must leave tonight after dark. Good luck!"

Just after nightfall, Janjo, Shika, the three soldiers, Gaston, Pablo, Anton and an old Swahili sailor dressed up like Arabs. They were lowered one by one in a basket from the top of the walls of the Fort to the beach below. Silently they made their way towards Mombasa harbour where they spotted a dhow suitable for their purpose. Two guards sat fast asleep on the stern. Without waking them, the three soldiers silently dispatched them overboard.

"I hope the sharks don't find Omanis too indigestible," said Anton grimly.

"Let's get moving before someone sees us," urged Janjo.

Soon they were underway leaving the port of Mombasa behind them. The sea was rough and Shika felt sea-sick. He'd never sailed before and he wasn't liking it at all. Clinging miserably to the mast, Shika wished he was back home in Janjo's bedroom. Luckily, there was a good wind and the huge sail billowed out in front of them.

"There's a storm building up," said Gaston pointing to the east. "It looks black over there. I can see flashes of lightning."

"The wind is strong," agreed the sailor unperturbed. "We should be there in twenty-four hours."

"I'll keep an eye out for pirates," said Janjo, thinking for the first time that maybe history was not so dull after all.

As the night wore on, the wind became stronger. After midnight it reached gale force.

"Pull down the sail or we'll capsize," shouted the sailor, but the soldiers were too frightened to move. Janjo leapt to his feet and began to haul at the canvas but the rain had made it very heavy. "The tiller's too heavy," shouted the sailor from the stern. "I've lost it."

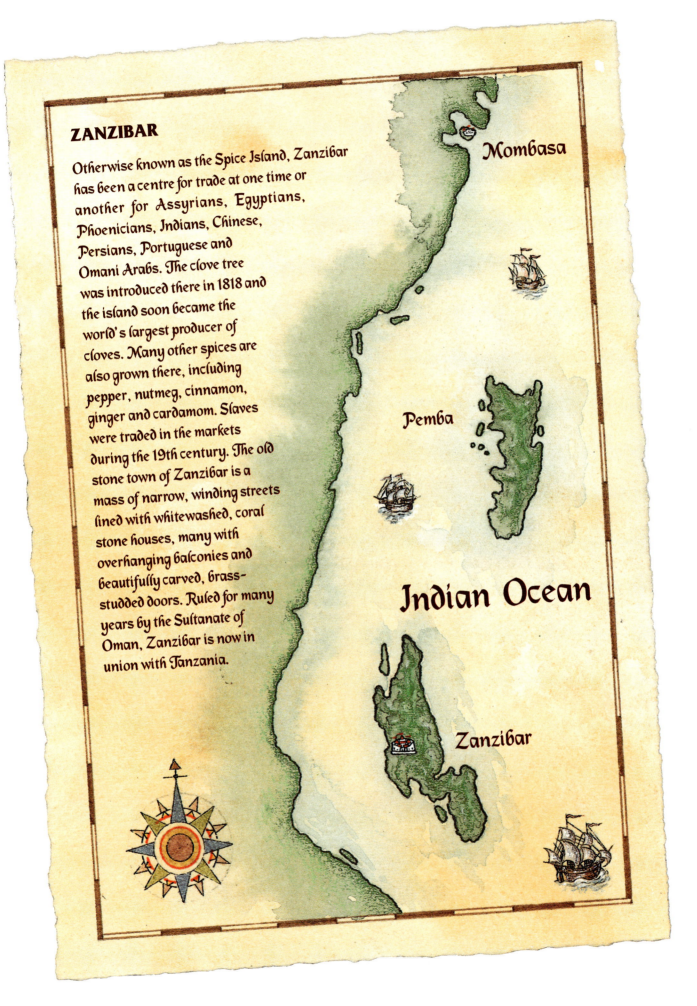

ZANZIBAR

Otherwise known as the Spice Island, Zanzibar has been a centre for trade at one time or another for Assyrians, Egyptians, Phoenicians, Indians, Chinese, Persians, Portuguese and Omani Arabs. The clove tree was introduced there in 1818 and the island soon became the world's largest producer of cloves. Many other spices are also grown there, including pepper, nutmeg, cinnamon, ginger and cardamom. Slaves were traded in the markets during the 19th century. The old stone town of Zanzibar is a mass of narrow, winding streets lined with whitewashed, coral stone houses, many with overhanging balconies and beautifully carved, brass-studded doors. Ruled for many years by the Sultanate of Oman, Zanzibar is now in union with Tanzania.

Mombasa

Pemba

Indian Ocean

Zanzibar

DHOW

Dhows have been used along the coast of East Africa and in Arab waters for thousands of years. The distinctive lateen sail is triangular and made of strong canvas. They may have a single mast, though the larger vessels carry a mizzen. The dhows are usually made from teak, one of the hardest woods available. The lower timbers are regularly treated against rot with a mixture of beef fat and lime, while the upper timbers are coated with fish oil to keep them gleaming.

There are two main groups of dhow and they are made in many sizes. Each type has a different name. The larger ones (Sambuk, Ghanjah, Abubuz, Kotia, Baghla) are often beautifully decorated with intricate carvings around the crew's quarters in the stern.

For over a thousand years Zanzibar was the terminus of the Arabian dhows which traded up and down the Indian Ocean coast. Nowadays Mombasa is a more popular harbour. Today their cargo consists mainly of dried fish, coffee, coconut oil and mangrove poles known as "boriti" used for building. Passengers can also be transported by dhow and although not expected to take part in the handling of the ship, they may be called upon to lend a hand during a storm...

As he shouted above the wind, the dhow lurched and keeled over on its side. The sea rushed in, flooding the dhow in seconds. Janjo and the soldiers were swept overboard into the raging water. Shika, jabbering with fear, hung on to the mast until he was blown away by the wind.

"Shika! Shika! Where are you?" called Janjo frantically as he tried to keep his head above the water. There was no sign of the little monkey.

"Help! I can't swim!" cried Gaston as he splashed about frantically trying to keep his head above the churning water.

"Over here!" called Pablo as the lightning lit up his waving hand in the dark. "Grab hold of the broken mast."

Janjo swam over to the heavy mast which had broken away from the dhow. He managed to grasp it and clung on desperately. Poor, poor Shika, he thought. What a way to die.

He must have dozed off, for when he opened his eyes again there were streaks of light in the sky. The sea was much calmer now and he could see that they were drifting towards a beach with palm trees swaying in the light breeze.

"Look, Pablo," he called out. "There's land over there. We're going to be all right."

Pablo looked up with disbelief at the long stretch of sand. "You're right, Janjo. Let's swim for it."

They pushed away from the mast and struck out wearily for shore. Finally reaching the beach, they dropped down exhausted on the white coral sand. The red sun of dawn rose over the horizon and warmed their cold, wet bodies.

Janjo sat up. "I'm hungry."

The last food he had eaten was some hastily cooked rice on the dhow. Looking up at the palms he could see clusters of ripe coconuts. "Come on, Pablo, let's break open a couple of coconuts for breakfast. I do wish Shika was here; I'm not sure I can climb a palm tree, can you?"

Pablo stumbled up the beach behind Janjo, their sodden Arab robes trailing behind them.

"You go first," urged Janjo. "You're taller than me."

Pablo looked up doubtfully at the swaying palm tree. He could see several monkeys jumping up and down and shrieking noisily for no apparent reason. "What's the matter with them?" he muttered crossly.

"Shika!" cried Janjo. "Look, it's Shika! He's caught up in that branch by his Arab robes. What are you doing up there, Shika? It's me, Janjo! Come on down this minute."

COCONUTS

Coconuts were of as immense importance then as they are today. From a coconut palm comes many useful products. The leaves are used for thatching, basket making and storage containers. The nuts' outer covering, copra, is used for fibre mats, ropes, etc. The milk in the nut is very nutritious a and the flesh is a tasty food.

Shika, who had used his Arab robes as a sail and been blown ashore, shrieked in frustration as he swung frantically to and fro in an effort to escape. With one final lurch his robe tore free and he bounded down the trunk and on to the sand. Then he flung himself into Janjo's open arms. Janjo hugged his lost friend, a big grin spreading over his face as the monkey fondly nibbled his ear.

"Stop it, Shika, you're tickling. Go and fetch us a couple of coconuts, we're both starving."

Pablo and Janjo stood side by side looking up into the palm tree as Shika scrambled quickly up the trunk and set about selecting the biggest coconuts. Just as he was about to pull one off, something whizzed past his ear and slammed into the shell of the coconut, knocking it from his grasp. Shika squealed in alarm and ran down to the safety of Janjo's neck.

"An arrow," gasped Janjo aghast. Before he could turn around, his arms were pinioned from behind and a sharp spear was waved in front of his face. Five African warriors armed with bows, arrows and spears, their faces daubed with stripes of white paint, stood menacingly around Pablo, Janjo and Shika.

"Look what the storm blew in," growled one.

"What shall we do with them?" asked a second.

"Let's take them to the chief," said a third.

The five warriors grinned delightedly when they saw Janjo and Pablo's horrified expressions.

The captives were led through the dense bush until they came to a small clearing surrounded by about twenty palm-thatched mud huts. A large, imposing man dressed in skins and adorned with colourful feathers sat on a carved stool outside the largest hut. An oval buffallo hide shield and a long, sharp spear lay in the sand by his feet.

"Kneel before the chief," Janjo and Pablo were told.

A discussion followed in a language neither of them understood. Finally the chief got to his feet, picking up his shield and spear he said, "My men will take you to the court of the Queen of Zanzibar."

Janjo and Pablo breathed a sigh of relief.

When Janjo, Shika and Pablo arrived at the court of the Queen of Zanzibar, they were overwhelmed by her magnificent palace. Gold, ivory, precious stones and magnificent carvings adorned the passages. Musicians played strange instruments, while veiled women danced around a fountain. The Queen lay on a couch, a snarling cheetah by her side. She was flanked by two huge eunuchs in red silk shirts and with dangerous-looking curved swords in their belts. Janjo, Shika and Pablo were brought before the Queen.

"What have we here?" enquired the Queen in a loud voice.

"We've been sent by Captain Rodrigues of Fort Jesus, Your Lady Majesty," said Janjo. "The

Omanis have laid siege to the Fort and many people are starving to death."

"Captain Rodrigues presents his compliments, Your Gracefulness," interrupted Pablo. "He badly needs your help."

"How do I know you speak the truth?" broke in the Queen imperiously. "You look suspiciously like Omani Arabs in those clothes. Perhaps you are spies?"

"Oh no, Your Royal Personage. These robes are a disguise which we wore to fool the Omanis when we escaped from the Fort," Janjo replied.

"Captain Rodrigues sent you this letter, Your Worshipfulness," said Pablo, taking a very wet and crumpled piece of parchment from beneath his robes.

The guards stepped forward thinking it might be a trick, but the Queen waved them back and accepted the letter from Pablo's shaking hand. She read it carefully, muttering and grunting as she did so. The cheetah growled, showing his long sharp teeth. Shika squealed in fright and hung on tightly to Janjo, burying his face in his neck.

"Hmm. Hmm. Very interesting," commented the Queen. She looked up at the two bedraggled figures kneeling before her. "Well, it seems that I must welcome you as my guests. Captain Rodrigues' appeal seems genuine and I welcome any opportunity to defeat the Omanis. I will send you home with three ships filled with food and ammunition."

"You are most kind, Your Most Worthiness," sighed Janjo in relief.

"Your help will be much appreciated by the King of Portugal," agreed Pablo with a smile.

QUEEN OF ZANZIBAR

Fatuma, Queen of Zanzibar was the daughter of Yusuf Mwenyi Mkuu. She was married to Abdulla, King of Otondo, and their son Hasan was to begin the building of the present day Zanzibar. Fatuma was given the northern part of Zanzibar by her father, while her brother, Bakiri, ruled the southern part. She preferred the Portuguese to the treacherous Omanis who she feared would block her trade with Europe and India in spices, grain and timber. Fatuma was later captured by Sultan Seif in retaliation for her help to the Portuguese in Fort Jesus. Sent to Oman to live in exile in for 12 years, she finally returned to Zanzibar in 1710.

Two weeks later Janjo, Shika and Pablo were back at sea, but this time in the company of three ships laden with a valuable cargo that included rice, flour, salt, spices, fruit, oil and sugar. Muskets, cannon, barrels of gunpowder and bags of shot were stacked below decks to keep them dry. Guards were posted at the hatchways to keep out thieves and the curious boy and his monkey.

"This food and ammunition will save Fort Jesus," said Janjo proudly as they came in sight of the Fort.

"I pray we are not too late," said Pablo in a worried voice. His wife and three sons were inside the Fort and he was missing them.

"Ship Ahoy!" came the cry from the crow's nest at the top of the mast.

The sailors rushed over to the side of the ship and stared into the distance. Sure enough, leaving the harbour, three large ships were coming their way.

"Omani ships! Ahoy!" yelled the voice again.

"Raise the flag!" shouted the captain. "Prepare for battle!"

The Portuguese flag was hoisted. A rumble below decks indicated that the cannon were being rolled forward in preparation for a fight. Sailors rushed to the stores to arm themselves heavily for the battle. They were in high spirits for they hated the Omanis. Any excuse to fight was more than welcome after two boring and uneventful days at sea.

A fierce battle ensued. Two of the Queen of Zanzibar's ships were finally sunk and Janjo watched heartbroken as the valuable stores sank beneath the waves. The third ship, carrying Janjo, Shika and Pablo, sailed into the shore beside the Fort.

"Well done, Janjo!"

Cheers of joy went up from all those watching from the battlements of the Fort as they saw Janjo and Shika on board.

"Quick, run for the hole in the wall," yelled Janjo as the Omanis continued to shoot at the sailors. "Get help to unload these supplies before they're stolen too!"

With a great deal of courage, the inhabitants of the Fort risked life and limb to carry the precious stores into the Fort. Finally, they were all stored away and the cooks began to prepare the best feast anybody had eaten in a long time. Janjo and Shika were congratulated and thanked by everyone.

THE FLAG

Not the Portuguese flag, but the banner of the Order of Christ, unfurled in honour of its former Grand Master, Prince Henry the Navigator. The flag bears a cross in the middle and a lozenge shape in each of the four corners.

CAPTAIN JOAO RODRIGUES LEAO

Renown as a brave and far-sighted man, he died of sickness on 23rd October 1696. It was reported at the time that his death was a result of his rage at the desertion of two slaves that he had particularly relied on to be loyal. Many such desertions to join the Arabs were then taking place for there was no firewood in the Fort and in desperation rice and other food was being eaten raw.

CAPTAIN ANTONIO MOGO DE MELLO

He was a former trader and the highest ranking civilian officer in the town. On 24th October 1696 he took command of Fort Jesus in response to the Viceroy's instructions. Because of the desertions and the fact that the Marakatos, Wangunya and Gallas people on the coast had all decided to support the Omanis, believing that the Portuguese would be defeated, Captain de Mello was eager to arm everyone in the Fort,

Rushing to greet Captain Rodrigues and tell him of their adventure, Janjo was alarmed to see an entirely new face behind his desk.

"Welcome back!" said the stranger, greeting them with a smile. "I have taken over the command of Fort Jesus. My name is Antonio Mogo de Mello. I'm sad to say that Captain Rodrigues died yesterday." Janjo groaned. He had admired the brave Captain.

"Cheer up. Now that you have brought us muskets and shot, we must teach everyone how to use them," Captain de Mello explained as he took Janjo and Shika to see the practice firing range. "It would be good for you to learn, Janjo. We need all the help we can get."

Janjo grinned broadly when he heard this. They'd kept him away from the guns on board ship, but he was keen to learn how to shoot properly like a soldier. He strode eagerly along beside the Captain as they approached the firing range where Pedro and Manuel from the kitchens were aiming their muskets at the picture of a turbanned Omani pinned to a palm tree.

"Not that way, you fool. You'll kill yourself!" yelled a shifty-looking soldier called Lourenzo to Manuel who was holding his musket upside down. "Although," he muttered menacingly, "That might not be such a bad thing."

"I think it's stuck," whined Manuel as he turned towards Lourenzo.

"Don't point it at me, fool!" barked Lourenzo as he wrenched the musket from the little man's grasp. "You're safer with a wooden spoon. Get back to the kitchens!"

Janjo practised hard and in a few days time he was using the musket with confidence. Shika made himself useful preparing the powder and shot and together they made a great team. Lourenzo made a mental note to watch the strange boy and his monkey carefully. They could prove dangerous to his plans.

On the 2nd November, Janjo was taking a stroll around the ramparts with Pablo when he saw something out at sea. Pointing excitedly, he yelled out: "Ships Ahoy!"

The remaining townsfolk rushed to the wall to see whether the ships were friend or foe. Captain de Mello was called. Through his telescope he saw the unmistakable flag of Oman flying from the masts of the eleven dhows sailing towards Mombasa.

Because of the increased threat to the safety of the Fort, many more people deserted over the next few days. Finally, Father Francisco drew the remaining force together to give them courage.

"Today is the 21st of November. It is the Festival of the Presentation of the Blessed Virgin Mary in the Temple. We must fire a salute of guns in her honour and show the Omanis that we are not afraid," he proclaimed.

"If we do that," Captain de Mello replied, "they will know how few of us remain in the Fort."

"What about if we put slow fuses on all the cannons and let them fire off one by one?" suggested Janjo. "Then the Omanis will think that we have more people and guns than we really do."

"Good thinking, Janjo," said the Captain. He gave Lourenzo orders to set the cannons around the ramparts. Janjo and Shika helped carry out the plan and soon all was ready. Just as the sun was going down, Father Francisco took his place on the ramparts and, in a voice loud enough for the Omanis across the water to hear, he began to pray. When he had finished he gave a secret signal and the slow fuses were lit. The plan worked to perfection. One by one the cannons went off all around the walls of the Fort, creating tremendous explosions. All the people shouted and cheered as loudly as they possibly could.

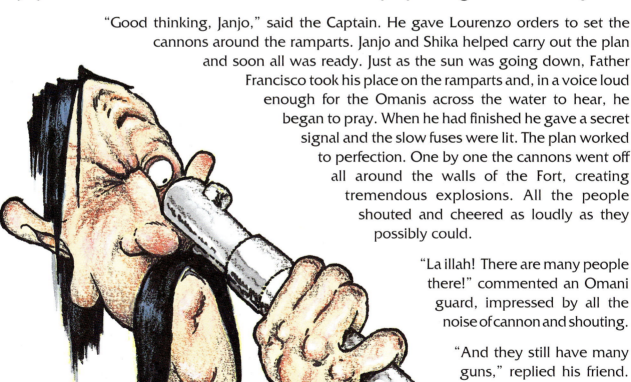

"La illah! There are many people there!" commented an Omani guard, impressed by all the noise of cannon and shouting.

"And they still have many guns," replied his friend. They rushed off to warn the Omani Sultan that defeat of the Fort would not be easy; their spies must have told lies about the number of people still left within the Fort.

For a few more weeks all went well. Then an unexpected visitor, accompanied by Lourenzo, arrived at the Fort and demanded to speak with Captain de Mello.

"Sir, I have come with a message from my commander, General Ali. If you surrender now, you and your Portuguese men are guaranteed safe passage back to Goa."

Captain de Mello stared at the Omani messenger who stood before him in flowing white robes and a tightly bound turban.

"Tell your General that I shall reply to his insolent message with gunpowder and shot, not with paper and ink. Not even the whole of Muscat will defeat us, let alone your pathetic force. Guard! Show this man to the gate and make sure he leaves immediately."

The Captain turned away and looked at the calendar. It was the 13th of December, and his supplies were growing low again. He was worried. Only about twenty Portuguese and 1,500 townsfolk were left after the sickness and desertions they had suffered. It was strange that only two men had been killed and three wounded so far during the siege, but now they could expect more attacks. The messenger would have seen how depleted the forces inside the Fort were and no doubt he would relay this information to his General.

As expected, the Omani onslaught now began in earnest. Access to the sea was cut off by fortifications that the Omanis built on the beach. When the Captain saw how a cannon had been erected in one of the trenches under cover of a roof of earth he commented: "That's devilishly well thought out!"

From the walls, the people watched as the Omanis began to construct scaling ladders to try to climb into the Fort. Janjo tried to help them think of ways in which they could repel the attack.

||||≡▲|||≡▲||||

Christmas Day arrived, but there were few celebrations.

"I wonder what my parents are thinking," said Janjo sadly to Shika as they sat in the kitchens after a miserable lunch of rice and stale bread. "I've never been away from home at Christmas before. Just imagine what we're missing."

A sudden volley of cannon made Janjo sit up with a start.

"What's that? Let's go and see, Shika. Anything's better than sitting here feeling sorry for ourselves."

Janjo raced up the stairs and up on to the ramparts to join an excited crowd. "What's happening?" he cried out.

"Look over there!" shouted a woman.

"They've come to our rescue," shouted her husband.

"Reinforcements!" gasped Janjo. "Shika, look! They've sent reinforcements from Goa. Hooray! Perhaps we'll have Christmas pudding after all!"

 Although the excited people waited all afternoon, the ships didn't come any closer, and finally it was evident that they had anchored out at sea. Everyone was very disappointed. They had all had visions of a fine banquet that night with the fresh food and supplies from the ships. Now it seemed they would get nothing at all.

GOA

In theory 'the State of Portuguese India' or Goa, began at the Cape of Good Hope and extended all the way to the Far East. Administered by a Viceroy or a Governor with his seat in Goa, officials in South East Africa received their orders from Goa and reported back to Goa, not Lisbon, the capital of Portugal.

THE RELIEF FORCE

Two frigates, two galliots and three large boats had set sail from Goa on 24th November 1696. They carried food and ammunition for the inhabitants of the Fort and were under the command of Commander Luis de Mello Sampaio. Unfortunately, most of the crew for the ships had been forced into service and none of them knew how to shorten a sail or navigate. Only the ships' officers had any naval experience at all. Having spent many days trying to find Mombasa harbour, they finally anchored some distance out to sea and refused to come closer to shore.

"Janjo, I want you to come with me to see what that Commander thinks he's doing," commanded Captain de Mello as he strode angrily down to the jetty. Despite the Omani defences, they were still able to get out to sea in a little rowing boat hidden behind some rocks. "You too, Lourenzo. Get your musket and come with us."

Janjo was about to suggest to the Captain that they go alone, without the untrustworthy soldier, but the Captain raced down the steps at such a speed that he had to run to catch up with him. Janjo just managed to leap into the dinghy as Lourenzo was pushing it off the beach.

"Wait for me!" he cried.

Shika had to hold on tightly as Janjo jumped over the side.

Janjo and the Captain sat in the prow, watching carefully for any movement on board the Goan ships. Shika took the tiller while Lourenzo rowed facing the prow. This meant he had to row backwards, which surprised Shika who had never seen anyone row like that before.

Without warning Lourenzo put down the oars. Stealthily, he put his hand under his robe and drew out a long, sharp kitchen knife. Shika's eyes opened wide in shock.

Lourenzo leaned forward into a half standing, half crouching position and raised the knife, pointing it at the Captain's exposed back. Quick as a flash, Shika pulled the tiller right round and the boat spun about with a lurch. Lourenzo was taken off guard. Unbalanced, he toppled over the side of the small dinghy and sank. "Help me! I can' t swim!" he screamed before sinking out of sight.

Janjo and the Captain turned round in amazement. Shika squealed and pointed to the long knife lying on the bottom of the boat, the blade pointing directly at the Captain. It was obvious what might have happened if Shika had not been alert.

"Well done, Shika. Quick thinking!" commended the Captain.

"I never did trust him, I thought he was a spy in the pay of the Omanis," said Janjo as he peered into the depths of the sea just to make sure that Lourenzo had gone for good.

Janjo and the Captain took turns to row through the dark night with Shika at the helm. About two o'clock in the morning the boat bumped against the side of the leading galliot. "Ahoy, there!" called the Captain.

A bearded sailor looked over the rail. He threw down a rope ladder and Janjo and the Captain climbed up the side of the galliot having first secured the dinghy. They were escorted to the Commander's cabin, a small but beautifully furnished room, where they waited patiently until he was ready to receive them. When the Commander finally appeared he was in full dress with lace cuffs, lace around the throat and a gaudy purple coat with highly polished gold buttons. He was not an imposing figure, with his fat red face, watery eyes and large belly, but he tried to make up for this by being loud and aggressive.

"Welcome aboard, Captain. Commander Luis de Mello Sampaio, General of the Relief Force of Mombasa, at your service, Sir. I have seven hundred and seventy men at my command, but most of them are useless as you have no doubt observed for yourself. We have no maps of this coast line and I have no intention of going any further than here. If you want what we have on board, then, Sir, you will have to arrange to pick it up for yourself." He finished this speech with a flourish of a lace edged handkerchief held to his nose in a disdainful fashion.

The Captain, a plain-speaking man himself, was appalled by the rudeness of his manner. "I am sure the Viceroy will be interested in your attitude to your position as General of the Relief Force," he said acidly. "I have risked death to come here tonight, and it seems you now wish us to put ourselves in further danger. However, be that as it may. With the help of fifty of your best men, I will take one of your galliots and another boat into Mombasa."

A plan was agreed. By noon the same day, the supplies had been loaded and the tiny fleet, comprising a galliot and a boat, was on its way. They approached Mombasa unchallenged by the Omanis, but when it was obvious that they were making for the Fort, the Omanis opened fire. The boat ran aground on the beach near the enemy position. Soldiers on the ramparts of the Fort, seeing their supplies under fire, managed to bribe some of the townsfolk to go out and refloat the boat while they gave them covering fire.

When the Goan soldiers and sailors on board saw the people from the Fort approach, they thought they must be Arabs. They panicked in terror. One thought to save himself and jumped overboard. Others, in similar panic, followed. With their heavy leather top boots on, many of them sank and drowned. The survivors struck out for the beach but the Omanis shot them down mercilessly. Others made for the other shore and found themselves in the enemy Omani camp where they were likewise butchered. Only ten men succeeded in reaching the Fort safely.

Despite being under heavy fire, the galliot with the Captain and Janjo and Shika on board managed to land on the beach near the Fort with only a few casualties. The galliot's cargo, mainly rice, was immediately off-loaded and taken into safe storage in the Fort.

"That was the most disgraceful affair of the entire siege," spluttered Captain de Mello in anger. "What fools those men were. Now we've lost another boat load of goods."

"Not so, Captain," said Pablo. "I managed to bribe some men to tow the boat to safety. We've got enough ammunition to last us a month or two. It cost us a few gold pieces, but it was worth every one. Now that we've got more rice and guns, we can last a bit longer."

"Pablo, I'm proud of you," said the Captain in relief. "You're a brave man. From now on you're promoted to my personal bodyguard. Congratulations."

Janjo and Shika shook Pablo warmly by the hand. He was a soldier they did trust.

In mid January 1697 Captain Luis de Mello Sampaio sailed away.

"The rotten coward," spluttered Janjo bitterly when he heard the news. "He only off-loaded half the food and ammunition he had been sent to deliver. I hope he gets fried in oil when the Viceroy of Goa hears about his behaviour."

"He's abandoned us," groaned Pablo.

Captain de Mello held his head in his hands. He was not feeling well. The tension and responsibility for all the needs of the Fort had started to overwhelm him.

Outside in the courtyard, Aldonca Gomes was tending others who were sick. She was the last Portuguese woman left alive in the Fort and had spent much of her own money trying to find medicines to treat the sick. When she saw the Captain emerge looking so pale and worried, she ran up to him.

"My lord, a strange and terrible sickness has come upon us. At least three people are dying every day. We have no effective medicine with which to treat them and I don't know what to do. They're swelling up like pigs' bladders."

The Captain strode over to one of the dead Africans whose chest had swollen up like a barrel. Beside him stood Manuel, shaking in terror, a large kitchen knife in his hand.

"Cut him open. Let's see for ourselves what devil inside has made this poor fellow die such a horrible death," commanded the Captain.

Crossing himself and shutting his eyes tightly, Manuel plunged his knife into the chest of the dead man. Immediately the swollen lungs and liver sprang out of the wound. A large black kite circling overhead swooped down and made off with the liver before anyone could stop it.

"I want to go back to Oporto," moaned Manuel. He wasn't feeling at all well.

The plague spread rapidly. Soon four or five people were dying every day and there was nothing anybody could do to stop it.

By the end of August 1697 Captain de Mello had succumbed to the sickness. As he lay on his bed, he spoke quietly to Janjo who was by his side.

THE PLAGUE

Plague is an infectious fever caused by a bacillus transmitted by the rat flea. Epidemics in human beings occur when there is an infestation of rats carrying these fleas. The disease in man has three forms: bubonic (infecting the lymph glands), pneumonic (infecting the lungs), and septicaemic (infecting the bloodstream). Plague is spread from rats to man in crowded urban areas. It is likely that the plague which infected the inhabitants of Fort Jesus was bubonic, causing the bodies to swell.

In the 14th century, when the disease was known as the Black Death, it has been calculated that nearly one quarter of the population of Europe (some 25,000,000 people) died of plague. Ships commonly carried rats, thereby spreading the infection in ports—like Fort Jesus.

"I am dying. The swelling sickness has caught up with me at last. I leave you in the care of Pablo. He, Manuel and two children are now the only Portuguese left alive in the Fort. When I am gone, Bwana Daud bin Sheikh must take over my command."

"But he's Muslim!" said Janjo in surprise. No Muslim had ever before been put in a position of trust by the Christian Portuguese.

"I trust him. His father was loyal to the Portuguese. Although Bwana Daud is only seventeen years old, he too is a good man." The Captain breathed with difficulty as he spoke. "Bwana Daud is well liked. Together with the other Muslims he will hold on to the Fort. I want you to call him now, my loyal Janjo."

"Don't die, Captain. Please don't die," pleaded Janjo.

Janjo rushed out of the Captain's office to find Bwana Daud. He found him playing with the two young Portuguese children in the courtyard. "The Captain wants to talk to you, Bwana Daud. Come at once. He's very sick."

They stood solemnly beside the dying Captain. With a great effort the Captain grasped Bwana Daud's hand. "Take care of my children. Take care of the Fort."

"I will my lord," replied Bwana Daud with tears in his eyes.

The Captain's body shook with pain. Letting out a terrible cry he died.

When the Arabs learnt of the death of Captain de Mello, they decided to make a full-scale assault on the Fort. The brave inmates of the Fort managed to repel the attack, thanks to the skilful leadership of Bwana Daud. But the battle exhausted them. For the first time they began to wonder how much longer they could survive.

The siege dragged on and on. Manuel and Pablo both died of the plague and Bwana Daud continued to do his best to stop the Omanis capturing the Fort. He became both the Captain and Governor of the Fort.

A new Commander, Captain Leandro Barbosa arrived from Goa. "I have been sent to take over control of the Fort," he said shaking the hand of Bwana Daud. "I understand you will be leaving for the court of Queen Fatuma in Zanzibar?"

"That is correct, sir."

"Are these all the people who are left?" asked the new Captain as he surveyed the remaining ragged and desperately sick inmates of the Fort gathered in the courtyard to meet him.

"I'm afraid so. Famine and disease have caused many deaths. We have fought the Omanis bravely, but many have been killed in battle," replied Bwana Daud.

The people were sad to see Bwana Daud depart. He had been a faithful leader and had managed the affairs of the Fort efficiently under very difficult circumstances.

"Goodbye, Janjo," he said. "Take my cutlass and use it to defend yourself when the time comes."

"Thank you Bwana Daud. I'll look after it and polish it every day!" Janjo took the weapon gratefully. He knew Bwana Daud had few personal possessions left as he'd sold his goods to buy food for the people.

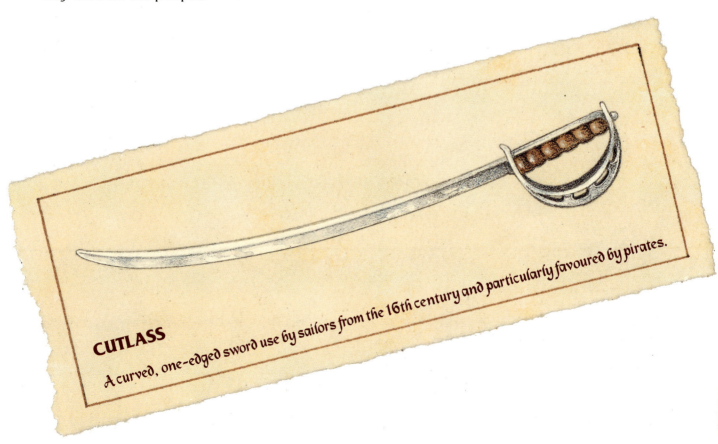

CUTLASS
A curved, one-edged sword use by sailors from the 16th century and particularly favoured by pirates.

On the eve of St. Lucia's Day, 12th December 1698, the Captain sent a young African out of the Fort to fetch fresh leaves to use as a dressing for a wound he had suffered in a brief skirmish near the Fort. The wound was festering badly through lack of medicine.

The young African was quietly edging around some rocks on his way to find the medicinal tree, when he stumbled over two Omani guards. They sprang to their feet and caught the boy by the arm as he tried to run away.

"Look what we've caught!" said one with a nasty gleam in his eye as he viciously twisted the boy's arm behind his back.

"We've a few questions to ask you," said the other Arab holding a scimitar to the poor boy's throat. "How many Portuguese are left in the Fort?"

The boy said nothing.

"How many are you?" asked the first Arab giving the boy's arm another painful twist.

"There are only eight Portuguese," sobbed the boy, "three Indians, two women, four Africans and a strange boy and his monkey."

"Is that all?" demanded the second man, drawing the sharp edge of his scimitar along the boy's stomach.

Too terrified to speak, the boy nodded. The Arabs threw him to the ground and cut off his head.

"They're finished," the first Arab laughed triumphantly. "We must tell General Ali to attack tonight before reinforcements arrive. Let's go."

General Ali was delighted when he heard the news. "One last push and Fort Jesus is ours," he exclaimed in triumph.

The attack began under the cover of darkness and was concentrated on the main gate and the wall on the shore side. Everyone fought bravely, but with so few men to defend the Fort, the Arabs easily forced their way through the meagre Portuguese defences. They surged into the Fort. Captain Leandro was mortally wounded in the battle and lay dying on the ramparts.

"The Captain's been wounded!" someone cried out.

"Look! Look at Saint Anthony!" cried someone else.

As the horrified defenders gathered around the fallen Captain, they saw the statue of Saint Anthony topple and fall from the top of the wall. It crashed into the courtyard below.

When the defenders of Fort Jesus saw that their patron saint had fallen, they surrendered.

"Quick, Shika. Let's blow up the powder room," urged Janjo running towards the tower. "If we can't hold the Fort, at least the Omanis shan't take it in one piece!"

Janjo attached a long fuse to a barrel of gunpowder. Five more barrels of gunpowder were stacked against the wall. Shika grabbed hold of the flint box. Crouching down outside the powder room behind a solid stone wall, Janjo struck the flint. A spark lit the fuse.

"Run Shika! It's alight." shouted Janjo.

BOOOM!!

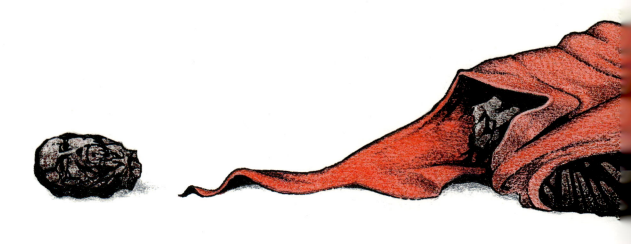

Janjo and Shika were
blasted out of the Fort by
the force of the explosion. They
were blown right back into their own
time and landed upside down on the floor of
Janjo's bedroom. A chair had fallen over and
Janjo's school books were lying all over the floor.

"What on earth is going on? What's all that noise?"
shouted Janjo's father angrily as he stormed into Janjo's
bedroom. "What's all this mess, Janjo? You're supposed to
be doing your homework."

"I'm sorry, father," answered Janjo in a daze. "I was pretending
I was in Fort Jesus when it blew up."

"Just look at the time," complained his father. "You've been in here
for two hours and it doesn't look as though you've done any work at
all. Your supper is ready now. You'll have to finish your essay after you've
eaten."

Janjo glanced down at his watch. The date was back to normal. "I wonder
what would have happened if I'd altered the date back to the present when
I was in Fort Jesus?" he thought to himself.

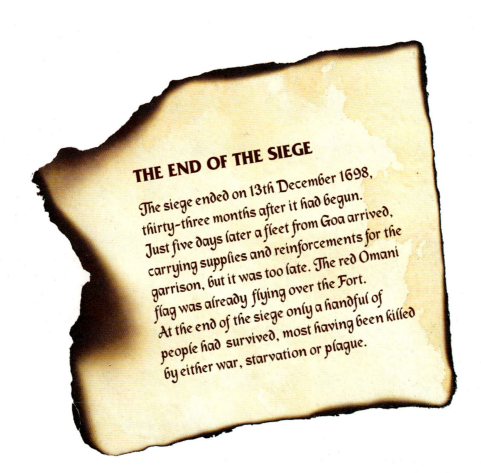

THE END OF THE SIEGE

The siege ended on 13th December 1698,
thirty-three months after it had begun.
Just five days later a fleet from Goa arrived,
carrying supplies and reinforcements for the
garrison, but it was too late. The red Omani
flag was already flying over the Fort.
At the end of the siege only a handful of
people had survived, most having been killed
by either war, starvation or plague.

Next morning Janjo handed a brilliant factual essay to his amazed headmaster. "This is excellent, Janjo. I don't understand how you've managed to get so many interesting details into your story. You write as though you'd actually been there at the time."

"Too true," muttered Janjo under his breath.

"What was that?"

"Oh, nothing, sir. I was just thinking how interesting history can be."

Where to find the *Fact Boxes*

EVENTS TO REMEMBER

1592

In Mombasa: Construction of Fort Jesus began.

In Spain: 100th anniversary of Christopher Columbus' search for a direct sea-route to the East in 1492.

In Japan: General Hideyoshi invaded Korea.

In England: In 1596 Sir Francis Drake led the second expedition to circumnavigate the world.

In India: Shah Jahan, Moghul Emperor of India, was born. He later constructed the Taj Mahal in memory of his wife.

1612

In Mombasa: Construction of Fort Jesus completed.

In America: In 1620 Puritan Pilgrim Fathers left England in the 'Mayflower' and founded New Plymouth (later Boston).

In Oman: In 1624 the Yarubi dynasty came to power.

In Canada: In 1642 the French founded Montreal.

In China: In 1644 the Manchu Dynasty came to power and ruled until 1912.

In Australia: In 1645 Tasman, a Dutch navigator, discovered New Zealand and Tasmania.

In Europe: In 1648 the Treaty of Westphalia brought to an end the Thirty Years' War.

In England: In 1649, King Charles I was executed and the country declared a Republic.

In Oman: In 1650 Sultan bin Seif drove the Portuguese from Muscat and made Oman a great maritime power in the Indian Ocean.

1652

In Zanzibar: The Omanis were invited to Zanzibar.

In Brazil: In 1693 gold was discovered.

1696

In Mombasa: The Siege of Fort Jesus began.

1698

In Mombasa: The Fall of Fort Jesus.

In Russia: A tax was imposed on the wearing of beards.

In India: In 1699 the 10th and last Sikh Guru, Gobind Singh, founded the Khalsa, an elite group of soldier-saints.

The Author

Dan Fulani spent much of his early life in the mountainous area between Northern Nigeria and the Cameroon Republic. Having spent some time writing and producing programmes for the BBC Africa Service, he entered the publishing profession and started to write readers and novels for Africa and elsewhere. He has had over thirty titles published, including a primary and secondary Hausa language course, and is the author of the well-known Sauna Series which has sold over 500,000 copies all over Africa and which has been successfully adapted into a television series. A number of his novels highlight specific issues such as anti-poaching, the dumping of harmful pesticides and the preservation of endangered species. He now lives in Nairobi.

The Artist

Patrick Kirby has lived in Kenya for many years and has developed a passionate interest in African wildlife and ecology. This has led him to many interesting artistic assignments, the latest of which are the map of the Aberdares National Park and a Marine Conservation poster for children. His work in Janjo & Shika and the Battle for Mombasa has been the result of much historical research.

Patrick has been awarded the Kenyan Award for Best Illustrator on numerous occasions and is one of the most sought-after freelance artists in Kenya today.

Portugal

Africa

Oman

Goa

Mombasa
Zanzibar